GOD IS GOOD

GOD IS GOOD

Developing a Good Mindset Towards God

Folake Hassan

The Righteous Publishing House

London UK

Copyright © Folake Hassan 2014

Unless otherwise stated all Scripture quotations are taken from The Amplified Bible (AMP)

All rights reserved. No part of this publication may be reproduced or transmitted in any form or by any means, electronic or mechanical, including photocopying, recording, or by any informative storage and retrieval system, without the written permission of the Author.

GOD IS GOOD

ISBN: 978-0-9928684-4-4

Published by The Righteous Publishing House

Flat 7, 93 Villiers Road

Willesden. London NW2 5QB

Visit Our Website at:

www.theblessedchristian.co.uk

APPRECIATION

I give all praises to God Almighty, who chose me and qualified me to be a Christian. I thank God for empowered me to study His Word and for blessing me with His Wisdom. My sincere appreciation also goes to the men and women from every part of the world that God has used to minister His Words to bless me. I thank my children for their good attitude that have enabled me to walk a good walk in my journey as a Christian. I thank my parents for taking good care of me through my childhood and they still do today.

Table of Contents

Introduction 1

[1]....Our God is the God of Special Revelation 7

[2]....The Lord Made All Things 17

[3]....The Lord Keeps Truth and is Faithful Forever 19

[4]....The Lord Executes Justice for the Oppressed 23

[5]....The Lord Gives Food to the Hungry 25

[6]....The Lord Sets Free the Prisoners 27

[7]....The Lord Opens the Eyes of the Blind 31

[8]....The Lord Lifts Up Those Who are Bowed Down 33

[9]....The Lord Loves the Righteous 35

[10]....The Lord Protects and Preserves the Strangers 37

[11]....The Lord Upholds the Fatherless and the Widow 39

[12]....The Lord Makes the Way of the Wicked Crooked 41

[13]....The Lord Reigns 43

BECOMING A CHRISTIAN 47

Introduction

God wants us to develop a good mindset towards Him and towards man. This book will encourage someone to start developing a good mindset towards God. God has been good to all humanity, God is not the source of evils. We should all remembered how God has been good to each and everyone of us and should not allow anyone or anything to make us to start developing a wrong attitudes towards God and towards the people He has used to blessed us. God does not caused evils to happen to anyone. Negative things may happen to anyone if they are ignorant of The Truth about God or about the situations they are facing. Hence, the reason why we must allow an abundance of The Word of The Living God to dwell in each and every one of us, fully and richly, as lamps unto our feet in all things. These we can achieved by choosing to study The Holy Bible on a daily basis and be a habitual reader of Christian literatures. To assist in this regard, please see my Website at www.theblessedchristian.co.uk for quality Christian resources that can enlighten your Christian walk.

Also, **I will recommend the King James Version of the Bible and other trusted translations for reading.**

The Bible advices us to:

> Study and be eager and do your utmost to present yourself to God approved (tested by trial), a workman who has no cause to be ashamed, correctly analysing and accurately dividing [rightly handling and skilfully teaching] the Word of Truth. (2 Timothy 2:15)

<u>We must all desire to know more about God.</u>

> But will God indeed dwell with men on the earth? Behold the heavens and heaven of heavens [in its most extended compass] cannot contain God (1 Kings 8:27); yet graciously in His infinite mercy; He comes down to dwell among us (His people).

God is Good, His faithfulness is without measure; God, despite His Majesty; despite who God is; He chose to come down to dwell among us and to attend to our needs. That is more than enough for us to know the awesomeness and the faithfulness of The Almighty God. God cannot wish anyone evil. God's plans for us are of good and not of evil. God will not bring tragedy on anyone.

I will recommend to everyone reading this book to use the attributes of God as a tool to:

**Pray and ask for miracles from God

**To meditate

**To accept each attributes personally

**To hold on to each attributes until they see its manifestations in their lives.

Also it can be used to put God into the remembrance of His Word and to remind us of the miracles of God. God says in His Word

> Put Me in remembrance [remind Me of your merits]; let us plead and argue together. Set forth your case, that you may be justified (proved right) (Isaiah 43:26).

**To remind us of whom God is and the rich inheritance we have in Christ.

**Also I hope it helps to develop, encourage and energise someone's faith and their trust in the Lord.

Our faith comes more alive and strengthened when we acknowledge who God is.

Whatever we call God is what He will become in our lives. It is good and rewarding to discover the goodness of the Lord and to do all within our abilities not to accept what the circumstances or traditions may be dictating to us about God; for example as Christians we must accept and believe that **God is a good God**; He is not the one who put sickness and diseases on anyone.

Also what I would love to achieve from this book is to see everyone reading this book to take, receive and believe each of the attributes personally for themselves and their loved ones. If possible, I will recommend that we all ponder over each attributes and accept them personally.

Also, this Book should encourage us to always thank God for Who He is, for the price He paid on our behalf; for His unconditional love for each and every one of us; for while we were sinners Christ died for us and He made provision for all that we will ever needs.

> But God shows and clearly proves His [own] love for us by the fact that while we were still sinners, Christ (the Messiah, the Anointed One) died for us (Romans 5:8)

Therefore let us all practise what the Bible says in 1 John 4:19 "we love Him, because He first loved us"

Once we discover who God is; we will know how to praise Him; we will know what to expect from Him

> Truly I tell you, whoever says to this mountain, be lifted up and thrown into the sea! And does not doubt at all in his heart but believes that what he says will take place; it will be done for him. For this reason I am telling you, whatever you ask for in prayer, <u>believe (trust and be confident) that it is granted to you</u>, and you will [get it]. (Mark 11:23-24)

And this is the confidence (the assurance, the privilege of boldness) which we have in Him: [we are sure] that if we ask anything (make any request) <u>according to His will</u> (in agreement with His own plan), He listens to and hears us. And if (since) we [positively] know that He listens to us in whatever we ask, we also know [with settled and absolute knowledge] that we have [granted us as our present possessions] the requests made of Him.
(1 John 5:14-15)

***Bible quotations in this book are from The Amplified Version of the Bible except otherwise stated.

<u>**The Scripture Reference for this book is: Psalm 146: 5-10**</u>

[1]

Our God is the God of Special Revelation

> "Happy (blessed, fortunate, enviable) is he who has the God of [special revelation to] Jacob for his help, whose hope is in the Lord his God" (Psalm 146:5a)

If you have prayed the Prayer of Salvation (see the back of this book, immediately after Section 3) then you qualify to be a Christian, and as a Christian you have entitlements to all the promises and blessings of God as stated in the Holy Bible. God is good; He will never leave His children and all His chosen vessels in the darkness or without a direction.

Have you ever been confused about any situations or felt in need of a special revelation and lights of direction from God concerning a challenge faced or may be facing? I will advise you to trust in the Lord, learn to dwell more on The Word of God; pray and ask God to give you the ability to study His Word regularly. At the appropriate time, as you continue to give attention to the Word of God, the Lord will lead you to the right Scriptures that will bring solutions to your problems.

I am writing this from a personal experience, the Lord has favoured me several times by leading me to the Scriptures that addressed my concerns at a particular time. I believe God can do the same for anyone that chooses to trust Him. At times it may take an instant or a while before you are connected to that kind of privilege or relationships where you can hear God clearly concerning all matters through His Word, but I can assure you; it will surely come as long as you continue to walk with God daily by studying and meditating on His Word.

The right Word or revelation you need concerning a situation may come instantly or deferred depending on how urgent the matter is. As the Holy Spirit continues to encourage you to stay in the Word of God, you shall surely be feed of God.

> Trust, (lean on, rely on, and be confident)
> in the Lord and do good; so shall you
> dwell in the land and feed surely on His
> faithfulness, and truly you shall be fed.

> Delight yourself also in the Lord, and He will give you the desires and secret petitions of your heart (Psalm 37: 3-4)

Concerning all things, concerning those breakthroughs; concerning those big projects; concerning the Salvations of our loved ones; **we all need Special Revelations from God, we all need to know what to do and what not to do concerning all things; we all need directions; we all need Godly counsels that are precise.** God, through His Words is capable of guiding us into all truth. God, through His Word is able to give us specific direction concerning all things. At times, the measure of time we give to hearing The Word of God is what will determine what we will hear, therefore we need to invest a portion of our time to continue to study and listen to the Word of God especially the ones from The Anointed men and women of God, knowing it may take a bit of time to arrive at our good desired results, but the good results will surely come as we continue to dwell in the Word of God and allow the Word of God to dwell in us, I pray that The Lord God will provide all the necessary resources we need to empower us to dwell on His Words more in The Name of Jesus Christ.

> So be patient, brethren, [as you wait] till the coming of the Lord. See how the farmer waits expectantly for the precious harvest from the land. [See how] he keeps up his patient [vigil] over it until it receives the early and late rains. (James 5:7) Also, see Matthew 4:26-27

Further assurance that God will instruct and teach us all things can be found in Psalm 32:8

> I [the Lord] will instruct you and teach you in the way you should go; I will counsel you with My eye upon you
> (Psalm 32: 8)

There are some revelations that are not common; they are unique, they are precise, reserved only for the righteous (those who are upright and in right standing with God); those who are diligent in seeking God. <u>Special revelations are to guard and guide the paths of the just and to preserve the way of God's saints.</u> (See Proverbs 2: 7-8)

Prayer: I pray that the Lord God of special Revelation will give each and every one of us the unusual miracles that will launch us into Everlasting Blessings in The Name of Jesus Christ. The Lord will lead us to the breakthroughs that will terminate all forms of shame and ridicule in The Mighty Name of Jesus Christ.

If you are a praying person, you can hold on to this Bible reference for this paragraph of this book (Psalm 146: 5a) and use it to pray fervently for The Lord God to give you Special Revelations; Divine Directions concerning a challenge you may be facing; concerning a good change you desire in The Name of Jesus Christ.

> Happy (blessed, fortunate, and enviable) is he who has the God of [special revelation to] Jacob for his help, whose hope is in the Lord his God (Psalm 146:5a)

Prayer: Pray and ask the Word of God to answer for you speedily in The Name of Jesus Christ just as the Lord said in Luke 18:8. That the Lord will give you special revelation concerning all

things in The Name of Jesus Christ. The Word of God to decree good things concerning you.

> And will not [our just] God
> defend and protect and avenge His elect
> (His chosen ones), who cry to Him day
> and night? Will He defer them and delay
> help on their behalf? I tell you, He will
> defend and protect and avenge them
> speedily. However, when the Son of Man
> comes, will He find [persistence in] faith
> on the earth? (Luke 18:7-8)

The secrets behind all the inventions, the innovations and advancements we see in our society today has been the fact that some people can see what others cannot see. God is favouring some people by showing them what others are not seeing; He is giving some people what I call "Divine Revelations". God is opening the eyes of their understanding. I pray that the Lord God will open your eyes to see The Special Revelations that will bring and establish your uncommon blessings in The Name of Jesus Christ.

In Bible times, it was usual for God to single people out to bless them by showing them the way they should go and the actions they should take concerning all matters; God is still alive, hence the reason for all the miracles and the blessings we experience daily; hence the reason for all the new inventions in our society. My prayer is that Gods presence will continue to increase in our midst to launch us into uncommon blessings for our lives in The Name of Jesus Christ.

Ask God to speak to you concerning those situations you are facing. Pray that the Lord will give you the hearing hearts to hear Him and to obey in The Name of Jesus Christ.

> So give Your servant an understanding mind and a hearing heart to judge Your people, that I may discern between good and bad. For who is able to judge and rule this Your great people? (1 Kings 3:9)

Some of the Instances in the Bible Where God showed Himself to be a God of Special Revelations

a. God revealed that the earth was without form, an empty waste; that it was full of darkness; and He did something about the situations by starting the creations.

> In the beginning God (prepared, formed, fashioned, and) created the heavens and the earth. The earth was without form and an empty waste, and darkness was upon the face of the very great deep. The Spirit of God was moving (hovering, brooding) over the face of the waters. And God said, let there be light; and there was light. (Genesis 1: 1-3)

b. The Lord helped Adam and Eve by revealing to them what they should eat and what they should not eat to avoid death.

> And the woman said to the serpent, We may eat the fruit from the trees of the garden, except the fruit from the tree which is in the middle of the garden. God has said, You shall not eat of it, neither shall you touch it, lest you die (Genesis 3:2-3).

c. The Lord revealed to Noah the idea that Noah should start building the Ark for protection against the flood.

> Make yourself an ark of
> gopher or cypress wood; make
> in it rooms (stalls, pens, coops, nests,
> cages, and compartments) and cover it
> inside and out with pitch (bitumen).
> (Genesis 6:14)

d. The Lord instructed Abram to go away from his country; from his relatives and from his father's house to the land God showed him (see Genesis 12:1)
e. The Lord God assured Abram that he will surely have heirs (see Genesis 15: 4)
f. The Lord revealed to Abraham the plan to destroy Sodom and Gomorrah (Genesis 18: 20-21)
g. The Lord guided Joseph throughout His journey (Genesis chapter 37 – chapter 42)
h. The Lord guided and advises Isaac not to go down to Egypt (Genesis 26: 1-4)
i. The Lord showed Moses a tree which he cast into the waters and the waters were made sweet (Exodus 15: 25)

j. The Lord advices Joseph not to divorce Mary; that the child she carried was from Holy Ghost (Matthew 1: 20)
k. The Lord advices the Disciples not to leave Jerusalem until He has endued them with power (Acts 1: 4)
l. Throughout the Bible God speaks to His people by giving them specific instructions concerning all things. (see Isaiah 30:21)

> And your ears will hear a word behind
> you, saying, this is the way; walk in it,
> when you turn to the right hand and
> when you turn to the left (Isaiah 30:21)

God is still alive, He is capable of giving each and every one of us A Divine Revelation that will distinguish us for an uncommon Blessings in The Name of Jesus Christ.

[2]

The Lord Made All Things

"Who made heaven and earth, the sea,
and all that is in them" (Psalm 146:6a)

Have you ever wondered who gives good things in life or where those things come from, or who is the Owner of the world? The Bible clearly states that it was God who made the heaven and the earth and all that is in it. May I encourage you that you should not allow any problem the room to overwhelm you; the Lord God is the giver of all good things; therefore there is no reason to be jealous over other people's gifts; ideas or blessings. The Bible tells us that all good and perfect gifts are from above, they are from the Father of Light in whom there is no variation (see James 1:17) God is not a respecter of persons, whatever your colour, race or gender, the Lord is the God over all, and He is able to supply all our needs. It is confirmed several verses in the Holy Bible that God the Father is the Creator of all things (Psalm 24:1; 50:12. 1 Corinthians 10:26). Whatever may be your need today, trust in the Lord.

He shall supply abundantly all your needs according to His riches in glory (see Philippians 4:19).

Some of the Instances in the Bible that shows that God made Heaven and Earth

> And God saw everything that He had made, and behold, it was very good (suitable, pleasant) and He approved it completely. And there was evening and there was morning, a sixth day (Genesis 1: 31).

> The earth is the Lord's, and the fullness of it, the world and they who dwell in it. (Psalm 24: 1)

> If I were hungry, I would not tell you, for the world and its fullness are Mine. (Psalm 50:12)

Prayer: **Our prayer should be that The Lord God will manifest His Words in our lives, His blessings and the truth of His salvations to become realities in our lives speedily in The Name of Jesus Christ.**

[3]

The Lord Keeps Truth and is Faithful Forever

"Who keeps truth and is faithful forever"
(Psalm 146:6b)

If anyone asks you who God is, I believe Psalm 146 of the Bible is where you show them how it is expressly stated who God is. (This is just one of the several places in the Bible containing references to the attributes of God). All throughout the Bible, there are numerous passages where God shows and manifest His Attributes to prove His Majesty and Who He is.

Whether the world likes it or not, truth still persists today. We will not all be lost totally because the Owner of the Universe, he Father God is not dead; He cannot be killed; He is Immortal; He is Eternal. He has the whole world in His hand; truth will not be perverted forever. On a daily basis souls are been raised who will defend the cause of Christ around the world, who will not be silent until righteousness prevail in our land (see Isaiah 62:1). Glory be to God

> For Zion's sake will I [Isaiah] not hold my peace, and for Jerusalem's sake I will not rest until her imputed righteousness and vindication go forth as brightness, and her salvation radiates as does a burning torch (Isaiah 62:1).

We thank God, the keeper of all truth and all information. There is no need to fear or worry about whether our information are safe with any individual or organisation, because God is the keeper of all truth. He is our shield; He has all our information in the palm of His hand. He will not allow our information to fall into the wrong hands in the Name of Jesus Christ. If you are a Christian especially a Born Again Believer, I congratulate you, because I can assure you that the Lord we serve is a faithful God. I pray that you will be able to keep your own side of the covenant by walking in the law of God by studying and obeying what the Bible says on a regular basis, then I can assure you that you and your generations will continue to be a beneficiary of the goodness, faithfulness and the mercy of God forever in The Name of Jesus Christ.

Prayer: What the enemies meant for evil, I pray that the Lord will turn them around to blessings for us in The Name of Jesus Christ. The faithfulness of God will abound in our lives forever in The Name of Jesus Christ.

More Instances from the Bible

> For I the Lord love justice; I hate robbery and wrong with violence or a burnt offering. And I will faithfully give them their recompense in truth, and I will make an everlasting covenant or league with them. (Isaiah 61: 8)

Prayer: We receive the Anointing for faithfulness to God and to man; we receive Divine Cleansing from all forms of unrighteousness in The Name of Jesus Christ.

[4]

The Lord Executes Justice for the Oppressed

"Who executes justice for the oppressed"

(Psalm 146: 7a)

We thank God who made us to discover that eventually there shall be fair justice for everyone, souls will arise miraculously to stop all forms of abuse; oppressions; depressions and harassments in our lands. The Lord will pour His Holy Anointing Oil on souls everywhere and they will kick against all forms of evils. The Invincible God we serve will argue our case favourably as promised in His Word in The Name of Jesus Christ.

In God, there is no partiality, with God there is no difference between the Jew and the Greek, it is the same God over all (Romans 10:12). Thank You Lord for You are not a partial God. Thank you for executing justice for all mankind, whatever the race; colour or gender. Thank You Father God for You are not a respecter of persons (Acts 10:34). For everyone who has confessed Christ as their Lord and Saviour, The Lord God will always defend and executes justice on their behalf. I am glad and I am thrilled in the sense that there is a hope for me and my family, no matter what we may have been through or going through, a day will come when The Blood of Jesus will speak good things concerning us in the Name of Jesus Christ. All truth hidden from us will come to light one day and our victory and vindication will be established in the Name of Jesus Christ and so shall it be for everyone who studies this book and their loved ones in The Name of Jesus Christ.

Instances from the Bible

a. The Lord answered the prayer of Sarah: (Genesis 21:2)
b. The Lord answered the prayer of Isaac and gave Rebekah children (Genesis 25:21)
c. And The Lord remembered Rachel and gave her children (Genesis 30: 22)
d. The Lord released the Israelites from the slavery and parted the red sea for them(Exodus 14:21-31)
e. The Lord promises to execute justice for the oppressed (Luke 18: 1-8)

[5]

The Lord Gives Food to the Hungry

"...Who gives food to the hungry" (Psalm 146:7b)

Crops can grow everywhere, I don't think there is a Nation or a land that does not have its own species of crops that can grow there, every land and continents has their own species of crops that will always grow in their land, therefore hunger and famine will not destroy humanity again, laziness and idleness will not destroy humanity again. Even now, the desert lands now find ways to nourish their lands to make it fertile to grow crops.

We should always be willing to cultivate our land at all time. I pray that The Fresh Oil of Divine enablement to cultivate our lands will rest on each and every one of us in The Name of Jesus Christ. Our education or prestige in the society will not be the stumbling blocks to stop us from cultivating our land, our education and our prestige shall not lead us into famine periods in The Name of Jesus Christ. My Biological Father was a professional Builder. Despite His busyness as a Builder, he never misses one year without cultivating his farm thereby contributing to the feeding of Nations in His lifetime.

Prayer: Thank You Father God for we know there will always be food enough for all mankind. There shall be miracle men and women who will be willing to cultivate their lands as did in the days of Noah (Genesis 9:20). There is hope for each and every one of us; hunger will no longer destroy humanity. The Lord God will breathe on our land to yield its best unto us in the Name of Jesus Christ.

Our land shall not waste; our crops and our cattle shall not die in the Name of Jesus Christ.

The Lord will give us the passion, excitements, energy, finances and the wisdom to cultivate our land in the Name of Jesus Christ.

Instances from the Bible

    a. The Lord provides drinks: Exodus 15: 25
    b. The Lord provides foods: Exodus 16: 4-14
    C. Jesus feeds the thousands: (Matthew 14: 21)

[6]

The Lord Sets Free the Prisoners

"The Lord sets free the prisoners" (Psalm 146:7c)

We thank God for the Hope we have in Him, such that whatever situation has had you imprisoned or crippled will not last forever. That is good news for me and for you; no ugly situations will have authorities over us forever. <u>The evil oppressions from satan will not last forever whether it be financial imprisonments, emotional imprisonments, spiritual or physical imprisonments; it will not last for ever</u>. Whatever the ugly situations you may have found yourself, believe it that one day, The Lord will set you and me free never to be bound again by any unnecessary situation in The Name of Jesus Christ.

I pray that the Light of the Word of God will continue to flow in our lands, to flow to us and to flow through us; so that no one will be imprisoned for ever in The Name of Jesus Christ.

We thank God for the justice and the freedom we have in Christ. I pray that our Government will allow more teaching of the Word of God in our society to set souls free and to stop all forms of crime in The Name of Jesus Christ.

We thank God, the Maker of all mankind who fights for our freedom daily.

We thank God for The Blood of Jesus that makes us free.

Thank You Lord God for there is hope for those who have been limited by circumstances in life. Lord, You set Joseph free by showing him favours everywhere he turns (Genesis 39 – 46) even in the sight of the jailer, you favoured Joseph uncommonly, Joseph family thought it was finished for him, but you turns things around for him by taking him to a greater heights by making Joseph to become the Prime Minister of Egypt.

The Lord God sets Joseph free from prison for him to take a higher and better position in the society that same God is still alive today to set His Own People free from all forms of unnecessary solitary situations in The Name of Jesus Christ.

Prayer: **I pray Lord God that You will set free everyone who find themselves in wrong locations, wrong situations, wrong relationships or among wrong associations either knowingly or unknowingly in The Name of Jesus Christ.**

In Your mercy, Lord God send and release your angels on assignment to go and set captives free in The Name of Jesus Christ; just as You released Paul and Silas free from prison (Acts 16:26), Lord let Your Name be glorified in our midst again in The Name of Jesus Christ.

Instances from the Bible

a. The story of Joseph (Genesis 41: 14)
b. Paul and Silas was set free from prison (Acts 16: 25-26)

[7]

The Lord Opens the Eyes of the Blind

"The Lord opens the eyes of the blind"
(Psalm 146:8)

Lord I thank You for Your promises to give sight to those desiring to see, both spiritually and physically.

I declare and I decree that I and my family will not lose our eyes; we will not lose our sight; we will not lose our vision in the Name of Jesus Christ.

We will be able to see clearly both spiritually and physically.

We receive the Spirit to discern between rights and wrong, we receive the ability to see and receive the blessings You have set aside for us.

We receive the ability to see and receive all the hidden riches of the darkness. Bartimaeus cried to God in the book of Mark, You restored his sight (Mark 10: 46-52), Lord, I pray that mercy and compassion will attend to everyone desiring such miracles now in The Name of Jesus Christ.

Also in the book of Matthew 9: 27-30, You Lord performed miracles and gave 2 blind men their sight instantly. I receive my sight now to see all that has been unnecessarily obscured to me in the Name of Jesus Christ.

Vision is very important, both the spiritual and the physical sights are both important. The Bible says that without vision people will perish. As the Children of God, we must trust Him for directions concerning all things.

Prayer: Lord God, restore mercy and compassion by giving back sight to Your people miraculously in The Name of Jesus Christ.

<u>Instances from the Bible</u>

a. Bartimaeus received his sight (Mark 10: 46-52)
b. The Lord restored sight back unto Saul who later became Paul (Acts 9:18)

[8]

The Lord Lifts Up Those Who are Bowed Down

"The Lord lifts up those who are bowed down" (Psalm 146:8b).

In the Name of Jesus Christ everything that has made our heads bowed unnecessarily gets their powers broken from today in the Name of Jesus Christ. Sickness gets its powers broken; poverty gets its powers broken; hatred gets its powers broken; death gets its powers broken (declare that all evil curses and all unpleasant situations in your life gets their powers broken, command and decree them broken in the Name of Jesus Christ, command them to lose their powers and grips on you now in the Name of Jesus Christ).

Instances from the Bible

a. The day the woman with the issues of the blood met Jesus was the day she received her healing (Mark 5:25)

b. A woman that was bent down for over 18 years receive her deliverance the day she met Jesus (Luke 13:11-13).

Prayer: Whatever power that may have bowed anyone of us down unnecessarily for generations gets their powers broken in the Name of Jesus Christ (amen). From today, I walk tall and I walk strong in The Name of Jesus Christ.

[9]

The Lord Loves the Righteous

"The Lord loves the [uncompromisingly] righteous (those upright in heart and in right standing with Him)" (Psalm 146: 8c)

Thank You Lord for when You look at me, it is Your righteousness that You see. I receive now the abilities and the enablement to be righteous before You Lord my God and to be righteous before men. Every Christian that walks in the will and counsel of God are all righteous before God. For the Spirit of life in Christ Jesus has set us free from the law of sin and death (Romans 8:2) and our righteousness is of Christ says the Lord (Isaiah 54:17)

***Is anyone going through unnecessary persecutions; rejections or hatred today? May I encourage you by letting you know that everything in life has its expiry date, and the expiry date for such afflicting spirit was set when Jesus rose from the dead and Jesus Himself said "The world cannot (be expected to) hate you..." see John 7:7a , Jesus Christ condemn hatred and death on our behalf. He said He has deprived the world of its power to harm us (John 16:33) that should make us free from all forms of hostile and abusive spirit. Jesus already paid the penalty for all our sicknesses. (1 Peter 2:24) The chastisement for our peace was upon Him. Glory be to God.

The days of your feeling inferior, unworthy or worthless are over in the Name of Jesus Christ.

Instances from the Bible

- a. The Lord saved Noah and his family because he walked in habitual fellowship with God (Genesis 6: 9)
- b. Abraham was righteous before God (Genesis 18: 19)
- c. Righteousness and justice are the foundation of God's throne (Psalm 89: 14)

[10]

The Lord Protects and Preserves the Strangers

"The Lord protects and preserves the strangers and temporary residents"
(Psalm 146:9a)

The Lord personally wants His people to travel from places to places for several reasons, for the purpose of making new discoveries and for their enjoyments. Throughout the Bible there are records of God's people travelling from place to places, example was the children of Israel travelling from Egypt to the Promised Land., The presence of God was always with them, guiding and providing for all their needs throughout, not because of the amazing jobs they did, but because God showed His faithfulness to them miraculously because of the covenant He had with them; it is in the Nature of The Father God to answer the prayers of His loved ones. The enemy can bring fear of travelling to places or all around the world for whatever reasons; I pray that the faithfulness of God will abound in our lives as we make the quality decisions to obey God's instruction in all of our journeys in life. I can assure you that there is no fear in Christ. All you have to do is to pray and confess Jesus Christ as your Lord and Saviour (Romans 10:9) and that will qualify you to be under God's Divine Protection always. He will keep you and all that belongs to you in the shelter of His wings. He will not allow your foot to slip; He that keeps thee shall not slumber nor sleep: (Psalm 121)

Instances from the Bible

a. The Lord heard when the Israelites cried when in Egypt (Exodus 3:7-10)
b. He reproved kings for their sakes (Psalm 105:14)

[11]

The Lord Upholds the Fatherless and the Widow

"He upholds the fatherless and the widow and sets them upright" (Psalm 146:9b)

The above passage is a fulfilment of what was written in (Isaiah 49:25b)

…….for I will contend with him who contends with you, and I will give safety to your children and ease them

And all your [spiritual] children shall be disciples [taught by the Lord and obedient to His will], and great shall be the peace and undisturbed composure of your children. (Isaiah 54:13)

Thank You Lord God for You will always provide helps for the widows and the fatherless. You will always raise helps for them. The Lord God will always set them upright. Thank You Lord for You will always fight their battles and win in their favours. You will wipe tears from their faces and comfort them on all sides in The Name of Jesus Christ. (Revelation 21:4)

Instances from the Bible

a. Mephibosheth was remembered by King David (2 Samuel 9: 1-7)
b. The Spirit of the Living God led a widow woman to Prophet Elisha who was able to help her (2 Kings 4: 1-7)
c. The son of a widow was resurrected by Jesus (Luke 7: 11-17)

[12]

The Lord Makes the Way of the Wicked Crooked

"But the way of the wicked He makes crooked (turns upside down and brings to ruin)" (Psalm 146:9c)

Prayer: Thank You Lord for the days of evil has finished in our land. Thank You Father God for not making crookedness to prevail in my life; in the lives of my family and friends. Thank You Lord God for destabilizing all forms of wickedness in our land. Thank You Lord God for not allowing the schemes of satan to work. Thank You Lord God for not allowing any devices of satan to work. Thank You God for overruling all satanic judgements and activities. Thank You Lord God for bringing all satanic works to ruin.

More Instances from the Bible

> I will go before you and level the mountains [to make the crooked places straight]; I will break in pieces the doors of bronze and cut asunder the bars of iron. (Isaiah 45: 2)

[13]

The Lord Reigns

"The Lord shall reign forever, even Your God, O Zion, from generation to generation. Praise the Lord! (Hallelujah!)"
(Psalm 146:10)

The Lord reigns forever and ever, from generation to generation. Praise the Lord. Father we says Your Words are yes and amen. Thank You Lord for You reign over all things, both seen and unseen. We thank You for Your love for us will have no end, no limit and no boundaries in the Name of Jesus Christ

The seventh angel then blew [his] trumpet, and there were mighty voices in heaven, shouting, The dominion (kingdom, sovereignty, rule) of the world has now come into the possession and become the kingdom of our Lord and of His Christ (the Messiah), and He shall reign forever and ever (for the eternities of the eternities)! (Revelations 11:15)

The Lord reigns in my life, in my home, in my businesses, in my ministries, in the lives of my children, in the lives of my families, in the lives of my friends. The Lord reigns in our lands. He reigns in the nations of the world in the Name of Jesus Christ (amen)

Instances from the Bible where God Reigns in the Lives of His People

- a. Then Moses and the Israelites sang this song to the Lord, saying, I will sing to the Lord, for He has triumphed gloriously; the horse and his rider or its chariot has He thrown into the sea. (Exodus 15:1)
- b. God reigns; Jesus is alive (Matthew 28: 5-6)
- c. And we overcame sin and death by the Blood of the Lamb and the Word of our testimonies (Revelations 12: 11)
- d. Throughout the Bible, it is shown that God Reigns in the lives of His people

**** See also: Psalm 104:1-28; Psalm 105; Nehemiah 9; Hebrews 11; Psalm 47:8

BOOKS AUTHORED BY FOLAKE HASSAN

God is Good

We All Have Reasons to Praise God

The Names of God

The Attributes of God

Coming Out of Bondage

Be Encouraged

BECOMING A CHRISTIAN

Becoming a Christian is not a difficult task at all. The Holy Bible instructs every mankind to be born again by confessing our sin and accept Jesus Christ as our Lord and Saviour by praying a simple prayer of salvation.

The Prayer of Salvation

Father God, I come to You in the Name of Jesus Christ. According to your Word in the book of Roman 10:9, which says "If you acknowledge and confess with your lips that Jesus is Lord and in your heart believe (adhere to, trusts in, and rely on the truth) that God raised Him from the dead, you will be saved.

I confess Jesus Christ as my Lord and Saviour, Lord Jesus come into my life and forgive me for all my sins. Be Lord of my life in Jesus name, Amen.

Congratulations if you have just prayed this prayer, you are now a Christian and you are saved.

You now have rights to all the promises of God in the Holy Bible.

I will advise you to read the Holy Bible and other Christian literatures regularly to build up your faith in the Lord. Also you will need a Word based church to attend regularly. Be part of a good local church that teaches Christian to grow in The Word of God.

*****Please write to us to inform us of your new decision you made to become a Christian and we will continue to offer all helps necessary for you to grow in Christ.

Remain Blessed

Yours in Christ

Folake Hassan (Mrs)

Founder/President: The Blessed Christian Centre

ABOUT THE AUTHOR

Folake Hassan is the Author of the books titled "The Attributes of God", "Coming Out of Bondage" "Be Encouraged" and several other books. She is the Owner of The Online Christian Bookshop named The Blessed Christian: www.theblessedchristian.co.uk . It is Folake's passion to see souls saved and confess Jesus Christ as their Lord and Saviour. Folake Hassan is blessed with 3 children with the youngest being 18 years of age at the time of writing this book. Folake and her children lives in London, United Kingdom.

www.ingramcontent.com/pod-product-compliance
Lightning Source LLC
Chambersburg PA
CBHW061514040426
42450CB00008B/1614